Distribution of Late Pleistocene Ice-Rich Syngenetic Permafrost of the Yedoma Suite in East and Central Siberia, Russia

By Guido Grosse, University of Alaska, Fairbanks; Joel E. Robinson, U.S. Geological Survey; Robin Bryant, Maxwell D. Taylor, William Harper, Amy DeMasi, Emily Kyker-Snowman, Los Altos Hills Foothill College, California; Alexandra Veremeeva, Institute of Physical Chemical and Biological Problems in Soil Science of the Russian Academy of Sciences, Pushkhino, Russia; Lutz Schirrmeister, Alfred Wegener Institute for Polar and Marine Research, Potsdam, Germany; and Jennifer Harden, U.S. Geological Survey

Open-File Report 2013-1078

U.S. Department of the Interior
U.S. Geological Survey

U.S. Department of the Interior
SALLY JEWELL, Secretary

U.S. Geological Survey
Suzette M. Kimball, Acting Director

U.S. Geological Survey, Reston, Virginia: 2013

For more information on the USGS—the Federal source for science about the Earth,
its natural and living resources, natural hazards, and the environment—visit
http://www.usgs.gov or call 1–888–ASK–USGS

For an overview of USGS information products, including maps, imagery, and publications,
visit *http://www.usgs.gov/pubprod*

To order this and other USGS information products, visit *http://store.usgs.gov*

Suggested citation:
Grosse, G., Robinson, J.E., Bryant, R., Taylor, M.D., Harper, W., DeMasi, A., Kyker-Snowman, E., Veremeeva, A.,
Schirrmeister, L., and Harden, J., 2013, Distribution of late Pleistocene ice-rich syngenetic permafrost of the Yedoma
Suite in east and central Siberia, Russia: U.S. Geological Survey Open File Report 2013-1078, 37p.

Contents

Figures

Tables

Conversion Factors

SI to Inch/Pound

Multiply	By	To obtain
	Length	
centimeter (cm = 10^{-3} m)	0.3937	inch (in.)
meter (m)	3.281	foot (ft)
kilometer (km = 10^3 m)	0.6214	mile (mi)
meter (m)	1.094	yard (yd)
	Area	
square kilometer (km^2 = 10^6 m^2)	0.3861	square mile (mi^2)
	Mass	
petagram (Pg = 10^{15} g)	2.2046×10^{12}	Pound (lb)

Distribution of Late Pleistocene Ice-Rich Syngenetic Permafrost of the Yedoma Suite in East and Central Siberia, Russia

By Guido Grosse[1], Joel E. Robinson[2], Robin Bryant[3], Maxwell D. Taylor[3], William Harper[3], Amy DeMasi[3], Emily Kyker-Snowman[3], Alexandra Veremeeva[4], Lutz Schirrmeister[5], Jennifer Harden[2]

Abstract

This digital database is the product of collaboration between the U.S. Geological Survey, the Geophysical Institute at the University of Alaska, Fairbanks; the Los Altos Hills Foothill College GeoSpatial Technology Certificate Program; the Alfred Wegener Institute for Polar and Marine Research, Potsdam, Germany; and the Institute of Physical Chemical and Biological Problems in Soil Science of the Russian Academy of Sciences. The primary goal for creating this digital database is to enhance current estimates of soil organic carbon stored in deep permafrost, in particular the late Pleistocene syngenetic ice-rich permafrost deposits of the Yedoma Suite. Previous studies estimated that Yedoma deposits cover about 1 million square kilometers of a large region in central and eastern Siberia, but these estimates generally are based on maps with scales smaller than 1:10,000,000. Taking into account this large area, it was estimated that Yedoma may store as much as 500 petagrams of soil organic carbon, a large part of which is vulnerable to thaw and mobilization from thermokarst and erosion.

To refine assessments of the spatial distribution of Yedoma deposits, we digitized 11 Russian Quaternary geologic maps. Our study focused on extracting geologic units interpreted by us as late Pleistocene ice-rich syngenetic Yedoma deposits based on lithology, ground ice conditions, stratigraphy, and geomorphological and spatial association. These Yedoma units then were merged into a single data layer across map tiles. The spatial database provides a useful update of the spatial distribution of this deposit for an approximately 2.32 million square kilometers land area in Siberia that will (1) serve as a core database for future refinements of Yedoma distribution in additional regions, and (2) provide a starting point to revise the size of deep but thaw-vulnerable permafrost carbon pools in the Arctic based on surface geology and the distribution of cryolithofacies types at high spatial resolution. However, we recognize that the extent of Yedoma deposits presented in this database is not complete for a global assessment, because Yedoma deposits also occur in the Taymyr lowlands and Chukotka, and in parts of Alaska and northwestern Canada.

---

[1] Geophysical Institute, University of Alaska, Fairbanks.
[2] U.S. Geological Survey.
[3] Los Altos Hills Foothill College, California.
[4] Institute of Physical Chemical and Biological Problems in Soil Science of the Russian Academy of Sciences, Pushchino, Russia.
[5] Alfred Wegener Institute for Polar and Marine Research, Potsdam, Germany.

Introduction

Role of Yedoma in the Permafrost Soil Organic Carbon Pool

First estimates of Yedoma deposits as a substantial soil organic carbon pool in permafrost regions were provided by Zimov and others (2006a), with a total estimated organic carbon storage of about 500 petagrams (Pg) of carbon (C). This estimate builds on a first-order assessment of the spatial extent of Yedoma deposits, derived from a small-scale map by Romanovskii (1993) from which a Yedoma area of about 1 million km^2 was calculated. Subsequent slight revisions of the carbon pool (Zimov and others 2006b) and inclusion in a panarctic synthesis of soil organic carbon pools (Tarnocai and others 2009) provide an estimate for the total soil organic carbon pool in Yedoma of about 450 Pg C. This amount is about one-fourth of the entire 1,672-Pg C soil organic carbon pool estimated to be stored in permafrost regions (Tarnocai and others 2009). Various studies noted the importance of such a significant soil carbon pool in frozen soil and sediments for the global carbon cycle and its potential vulnerability to thaw, decomposition, and greenhouse-gas release in a warming Arctic where permafrost is projected to thaw across large regions (Walter and others, 2006; Schuur and others, 2008; Kuhry and others, 2010; McGuire and others, 2010; Grosse and others, 2011; Harden and others, 2012). Tarnocai and others (2009) and Schirrmeister and others (2011a) also cautioned about large uncertainties in the carbon pool estimates for Yedoma deposits because of limited field data on organic carbon content, distribution, and character; ground ice content; bulk density; and the spatial extent of these deposits. Enhancement of knowledge about the spatial distribution of the Yedoma deposits is a critical step in better assessing the total carbon pool in Yedoma deposits and its thaw vulnerability in different regions.

In this project, we focus on reducing uncertainty in the spatial extent of the Yedoma deposits by creating a digital geospatial database of Yedoma coverage in which we extract relevant information from Quaternary geological maps at the scale 1:1,000,000. This geodatabase will (1) serve as a core database for future refinements of Yedoma distribution in additional regions, and (2) provide a starting point to revise the size of deep but thaw-vulnerable permafrost carbon pools in the Arctic based on surface geology and the distribution of cryolithofacies types at high spatial resolution.

Yedoma Research and Terminology

Studies in Siberia

Yedoma deposits were first studied in Russia, where these deposits occur most extensively in the northern, central, and eastern Siberian lowlands. Originally, the term "Ice Complex", or in Russian "Ledovoy Komplex", was used to describe these deposits in reference to their very high ground-ice content when compared to other permafrost deposits (fig. 1).The ground ice consists of very large syngenetic ice wedges and intrasedimentary ice, such as small centimeter-scale ice lenses and horizontal ice bands. The term "Yedoma" was originally used to describe the hill-like landforms where Ice Complex deposits occur. More recently, "Yedoma" has been widely used and accepted for the deposits themselves, although many researchers also continue to use the term "Ice Complex" for these and similar ice-rich deposits in other stratigraphic positions, specifically in Siberia.

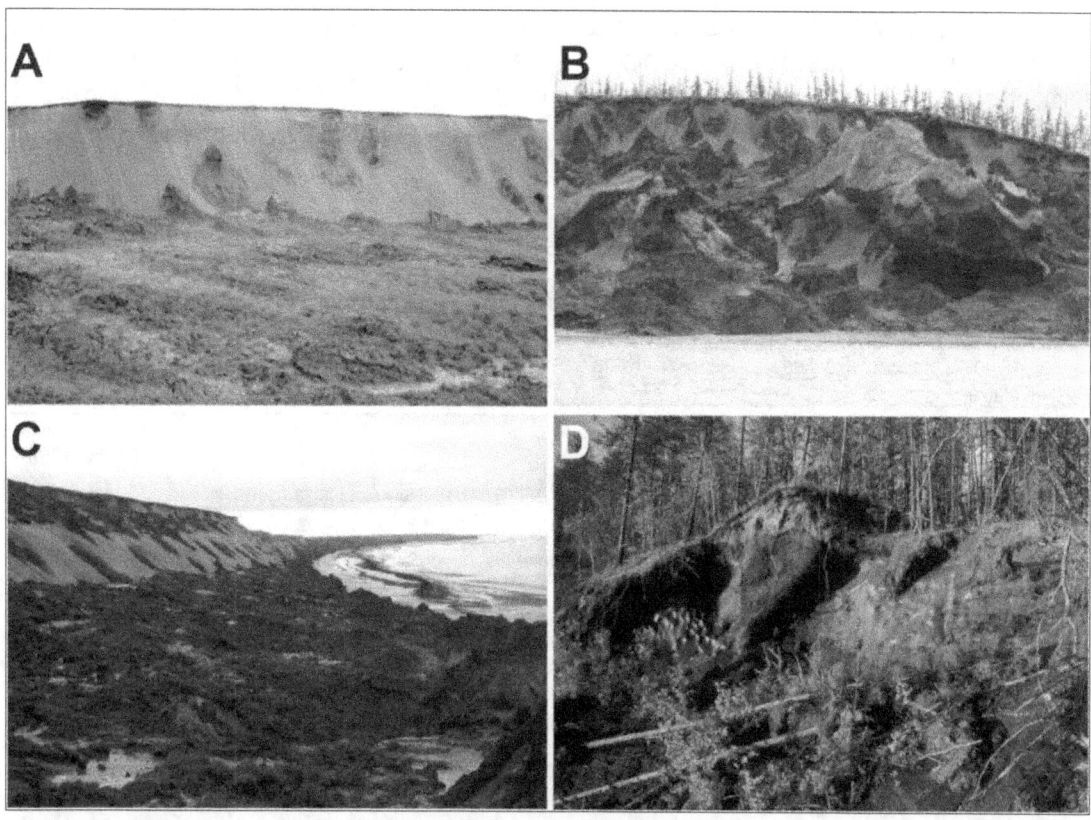

Figure 1.   Photographs showing typical Yedoma deposits with substantial ground-ice content and very large syngenetic ice wedges, Siberia, Russia. A, Bol'shoy Lyakhovsky Island, New Siberian Islands (Photograph by G. Grosse, 1999); B, DuvannyYar, Kolyma River, Northeast Yakutia (Photograph by G. Grosse, 2007); C, Cape Mamontov Klyk, Anabar-Olenek interfluve, Western Laptev Sea coastal lowland (Photograph by G. Grosse, 2003); D, Mamontovaya Gora, Aldan River, Central Yakutia (Photograph by L. Schirrmeister, 2001).

The first descriptions of Yedoma deposits range back as far as the late 19th century, when Russian explorers of the northeastern Siberian Arctic described these deposits as buried glacial ice remnants of extensive glaciations of the Arctic shelves, because of the large amounts of ice and small amounts of sediment that were observed in exposures on coastal and river bluffs (von Toll, 1895). It was recognized later that the observed deposits were of periglacial rather than glacial origin and that the ice actually formed as ice wedges and segregated ice lenses synchronously with sediment accumulation, also referred to as syngenetic ice. Since the mid-20th century, a wide range of geological, geocryological, stratigraphical, geochronological, biogeochemical, and paleoenvironmental research on Siberian Yedoma has been done by Russian researchers (for example, Popov, 1953; Vtyurin and others, 1957; Romanovskii, 1958, 1977; Ivanov, 1972; Katasonov, 1975; Tomirdiaro, 1980; Kaplina, 1981; Tomirdiaro and others, 1984; Konishchev, 1987; Tomirdiaro and Chernenky, 1987; Sher, 1997; Sher and others, 2005; Kunitsky, 2007; Streletskaya and others, 2007; Veremeeva and Gubin, 2009) and international research teams (for example, Péwé and others, 1977; Péwé and Journaux, 1983; Kienel and others, 1999; Siegert and others, 2000; Schirrmeister and others, 2001, 2002, 2003, 2008, 2011a, 2011b; Kunitsky and others, 2002; Meyer and others, 2002a, 2002b; Hubberten and others, 2004; Zimov and others, 2006a, 2006b; Grosse and others, 2007; Walter and others, 2007; Andreev and others, 2009; Wetterich and others, 2008, 2011; Strauss and others, 2012). However, some controversies on the genesis of Yedoma deposits, occurring in extensive regions with a wide range of modern environmental and permafrost conditions, have remained until now. Hypotheses on

Yedoma formation evolving from local or regional studies often were extrapolated to the entire Yedoma region and included deposition as eolian loess, flood plain or fluvial sediments, lacustrine and bog deposits, niveo-eolian sediments, proluvial slope deposits, and swamp deposits of large lakes dammed by shelf ice glaciers (table 1).

Table 1. Various historical hypotheses on Yedoma origin in Siberia, Russia (adapted after Siegert and others, 1999).

Origin	Suggested stratigraphy	Studied region	Citation
Glacial and glacial-related			
Buried remnants of glaciers		Bol'shoy Lyakhovsky Island, North Siberian coastal lowland	von Toll (1895)
Proglacial deposits of basins dammed by a shelf glacier	Late Pleistocene	Bykovsky Peninsula, North Siberian coastal lowland	Grosswald (1998)
Fluvial and fluvial-related			
River floodplain sediments	Middle Pleistocene	Lower Yana River	Popov (1953, 1969)
Giant icings with mud flow channels	Late Pleistocene	Bykovsky Peninsula, North Siberian coastal lowland	Gusev (1958)
Fluvial sediments of meandering rivers	(Middle)-Late Pleistocene	North Siberian coastal lowland, Lower Yana River, Bol'shoy Lyakhovsky Island	Vtyurin and others (1957), Romanovskii (1958), Katasonov (1975)
Sediments of a fluvio-lacustrine plain	Kargin interglacial	North Siberian coastal lowland	Strelkov (1960)
Fluvial (shallow channel facies)	Vorontsov Formation – Middle Pleistocene	Lower Indigirka River	Lavrushin (1962)
Alluvial-proluvial* / fluvial		Kular Range	Gravis (1997)
Lacustrine and swamp			
Lacustrine-palustrine sediments	Oyagoss Formation - (Middle)-Late Pleistocene	North Siberian coastal lowland	Kayalaynen and Kulakov (1966)
Fluvial and fluvio-lacustrine sediments	Oyagoss Formation (Zyryan)	North Siberian coastal lowland	Ivanov (1972)
Sediments of river deltas and swamps dammed by a shelf ice sheet	Kargin Interglacial	Bykovsky Peninsula, Bol'shoy Lyakhovsky Island, Oyagoss Yar	Nagaoka (1994)
Eolian			
Cryogenic-eolian ("loess ice") formation	Late Pleistocene	Bykovsky Peninsula, Oyagoss Yar, Duvanny Yar	Tomirdiaro and others (1984), Velichko and others (1984), Zimov and others (2006a)
Loess and retransported loess	Late Pleistocene	Lena-Aldan region, central Yakutia	Péwé and others (1977), Péwé and Journaux (1983)
Polygenetic			
Polygenetic origin (fluvial, slope, eolian, and so on)	Yedoma Formation / Superhorizon, subdivided into Oyagoss (=Zyryan), Molotkov (=Kargin), and Sartan Horizon	North Siberian coastal lowland	Sher and others, 1987
Polygenetic origin, but closely related to nival weathering, transport, and accumulation processes	Late Pleistocene	Laptev Sea region	Schirrmeister and others (2011b)
Nival			
Nival deposits (nival-eolian, nival-fluvial, nival-solifluction) (sediments delivered from seasonal melt of extensive snow patches)	Late Pleistocene	Bykovsky Peninsula, Bol'shoy Lyakhovsky Island	Kunitsky (1989), Kunitsky and others (2002), Kunitsky (2007), Galabala (1997)

Floodplains and slope			
Floodplain sediments, proluvial[1] slope sediments	Lower Ice Complex (Middle-Late Pleistocene) and Upper Ice Complex (Sartan)	Bykovsky Peninsula	Slagoda (1991, 1993)
Slope deposits	Late Pleistocene	Kular Range	Gravis (1969)

[1]Proluvial deposition, commonly used in Russian geologic literature, summarizes alluvial fan deposition in hillslope or mountainous setting.

Studies in North America

Yedoma also is known to occur in northwestern North America, where Yedoma-type deposits have been identified and described as frozen loess, windblown or re-transported ice-rich silt, or muck (for example, Péwé, 1955, 1975; Taber, 1958; Carter, 1988; Hamilton and others, 1988; Kotler and Burn, 2000; Shur and others, 2004; Sanborn and others, 2006; Froese and others, 2009; Kanevskiy and others, 2011).If these specific deposits are of late-Pleistocene stratigraphy and have indicators of syngenetic permafrost growth, they can be considered paleoenvironmentally and stratigraphically equivalent to the Siberian Yedoma (Kanevskiy and others, 2011; Schirrmeister and others, 2013).

Current Definitions of Yedoma

Sher (1995) established the view that Yedoma deposits are of polygenetic origin including fluvial, lacustrine, eolian, and slope sedimentation, but clearly excluded sediments of glacial and marine genesis. More recently, Kunitsky and others (2002) and Kunitsky (2007) showed that nival-eolian processes were important for Yedoma formation in the periglacial lowlands of northern Siberia. A critical factor for determining whether these different sedimentary facies types are part of the Yedoma Suite is whether they experienced syngenetic ice wedge growth and substantial ground ice accumulation during the late Pleistocene. Substantial new knowledge on various sedimentological, cryological, paleoecological, and geochronological characteristics of Yedoma has resulted from Russian-German research collaborations in the Laptev Sea Yedoma region (Hubberten and others, 2004; Schirrmeister and others, 2011b). Extensive radiocarbon dating of fossil plant and animal remains and luminescence dating of sediments during the last two decades corroborate the geochronologic and stratigraphic position of Yedoma within the late Pleistocene glacial period. Some of the earliest Yedoma deposits were identified on the Bykovsky Peninsula with ages around 60,000–70,000 years before present (BP), and their accumulation ending with the onset of Lateglacial and Holocene warming (for example, Schirrmeister and others, 2001; Sher and others, 2005; Grosse and others, 2007).

Yedoma differs from other permafrost deposits by the presence of large syngenetic ice wedges (Romanovskii, 1993; Meyer and others, 2002a; Shur and others, 2004; Kanevskiy and others, 2011), its substantial excess ice content (Kanevskiy and others, 2011; Schirrmeister and others, 2011b), and cryogenic sediment textures and structures (Konishchev, 1981; Konishchev and Rogov, 1993) suggesting lowland or slope sedimentation and gradual freezing processes.

Yedoma lithologies indicate intense periglacial weathering and transportation processes that often are associated with local low mountain ranges (Siegert and others, 2000; Schirrmeister and others, 2011b). An important process of sediment alteration in the Yedoma deposits is in-place cryogenic weathering, which is closely associated with harsh periglacial climates and seasonal nival processes (Konishchev, 1981). Yedoma deposits only occur in regions that were previously unglaciated during the late Quaternary (Sher, 1995; Hubberten and others, 2004), such as northeastern Siberian shelf lowlands, central Yakutian lowlands, and interior Alaska. Biogenic and abiogenic paleo-climate proxies in Yedoma indicate extreme continental climate conditions during its formation (low precipitation, very cold winters, and relatively warm summers), and the composition of biogenic proxies (remains of pollen, plant macrofossils, insects, as well as mammals of the mammoth fauna) indicate a dense mosaic of dry and wet habitats with polygonal-patterned ground in a generally tundra-steppe-like environment without modern analogue (for example, Sher and others, 2005).

Schirrmeister and others (2013) attempted to advance the definition of Yedoma by summarizing regional characteristics in northern, central, and eastern Siberia; Alaska; and northwestern Canada, and by uniting the previous scholarly views on Yedoma-type deposits across these regions (table 2).

Table 2. Key characteristics of Yedoma deposits in Siberia, Russia, and northwestern North America (adapted from Schirrmeister and others, 2013).

	Northern, central, and eastern Siberia (Western Beringia)	Alaska and Yukon (Eastern Beringia)
Earlier terminology	Ice Complex, Yedoma Suite	"Muck" deposits or syngenetic late Pleistocene perennially-frozen ice-rich silts
Distribution	East Siberian Arctic lowlands and large river valleys, foothills	Foothills and lowlands in northern and northwestern Alaska; unglaciated valleys in interior Yukon and Alaska
Sediment	Poorly sorted, organic-rich silt and silty sand	Organic-rich silt and silty sand
Genesis	Syngenetic permafrost of multiple origins depending on region: nival, alluvial, proluvial, colluvial, sheet-flow, soil-creep or eolian sedimentation	Largely eolian sedimentation (airfall loess) with syngenetic permafrost, locally redeposited and interbedded with other deposits
Formation age	80,000 to 12,000 years before present	
Stratigraphy	Marine Isotope Stages 4 to 2	
Landscape	Stable, poorly drained areas with low topographic gradient	
Paleoclimate	Highly continental, cold-arid	
Ground ice	Ice-saturated or supersaturated, syngenetic ice wedges, segregation ice	
Paleoecology	Tundra steppe-Mammoth steppe, cryoxeric vegetation, Mammoth fauna	

Previous Maps of Yedoma Distribution

Various maps of Yedoma distribution exist in the literature; however, most of them are small-scale (1:10,000,000 or smaller) maps that tend to generalize the spatial extent of Yedoma. A Yedoma map most widely referred to is that of Romanovskii (1993) (fig.2). The area covered by Yedoma in this map is 1,141,390 km^2. This map has been subsequently adapted by Siegert and Romanovskii (1996) and was then published in Schirrmeister and others (2002), showing Yedoma extent in central and northeastern Siberian lowlands and indicates Yedoma occurrences in formerly unglaciated valleys. Based on the Romanovskii (1993) map, Zimov and others (2006) estimated that the Yedoma area covers approximately 1 million km^2 of Siberia, an extent that was subsequently used to quantify soil organic carbon storage in Yedoma (Zimov and others, 2006) and the release of methane from thermokarst lakes during the Pleistocene-Holocene transition (Walter and others, 2007).

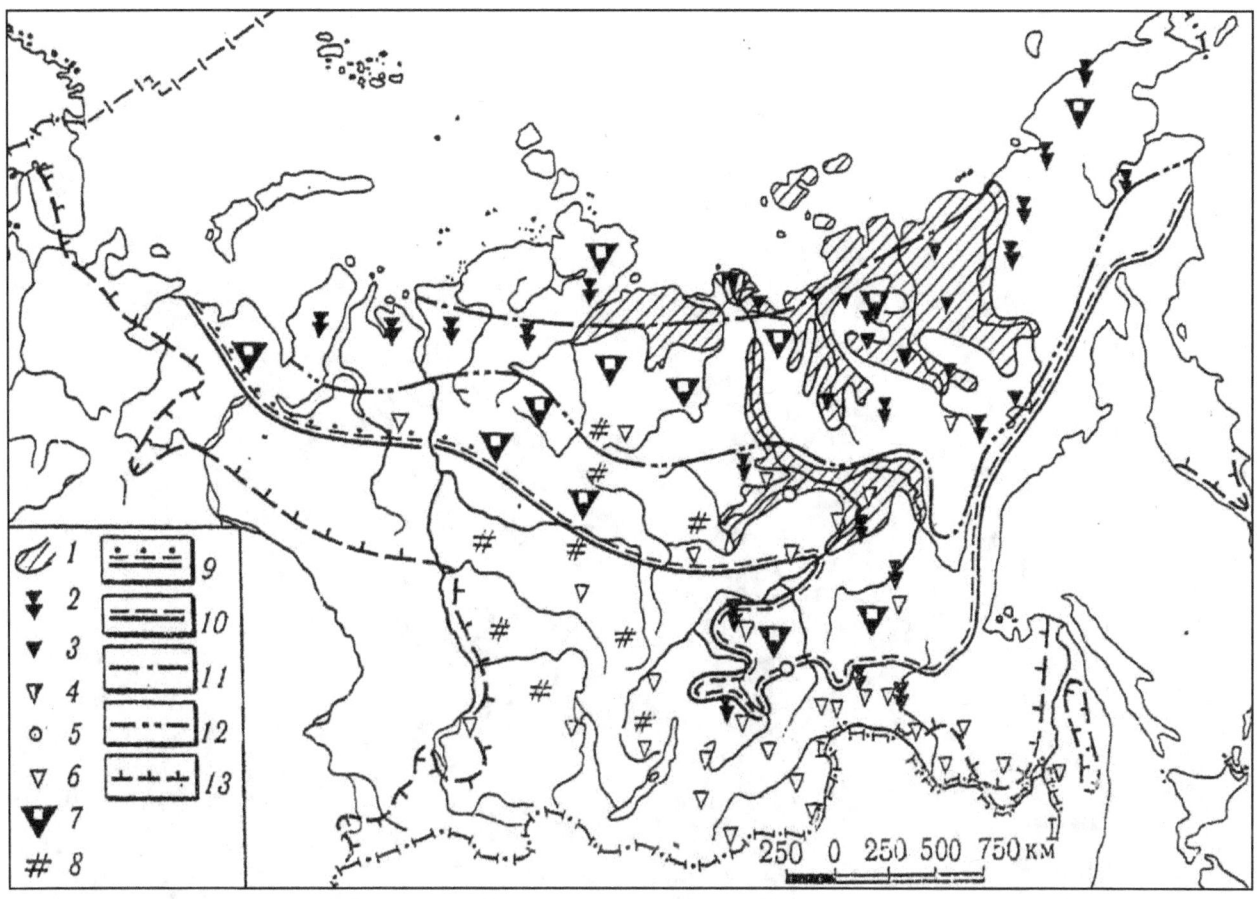

Figure 2. Schematic map showing Yedoma extent in Siberia, Russia (Romanovskii, 1993). 1, Region of wide distribution of "Ice Complex" (Yedoma); 2, Yedoma distribution in river valleys; 3, Active ice wedges; 4, Active sand-ice wedges (low-temperature); 5, Active sand-ice wedges (high-temperature); 6, Active ground wedges; 7, Sorted polygons; 8, Small diameter polygonal ground (1.5–3.0 meters); 9, Boundaries of active ice wedge occurrence in peats, 10, in sandy silts and silty sands, and 11, in coarse grained sands, gravels, and pebbles; 12, Southern boundaries of low-center polygons and 13, of permafrost.

In another recent adaptation of the small-scale map of Yedoma distribution, Konishchev (2011) separated the Yedoma deposits into three categories of spatial distribution, ranging from *widely distributed* to *fragmented* to *sporadic* (fig. 3). Several maps of regional Yedoma extent exist, scattered in the Russian scientific literature, for example, for the Yana-Indigirka-Kolyma lowlands (Tomirdiaro, 1980) or Yakutia (Grigoriev and Kunitsky, 2000). Field studies and high-resolution satellite imagery clearly indicate that Yedoma cover in the Yedoma region of northern Siberia is not uniform but can range from complete to fragmented remnants. For example, Grosse and others (2006) indicate that only about 22 percent of the Yedoma area in the Lena Anabar lowland near Cape Mamontov Klyk was not affected by permafrost degradation owing to thermokarst and thermo-erosion. This fragmentation in Yedoma extent is not represented in small-scale maps (figs. 2 and 3), but is captured in high-resolution scales of 1:1,000,000 and better.

7

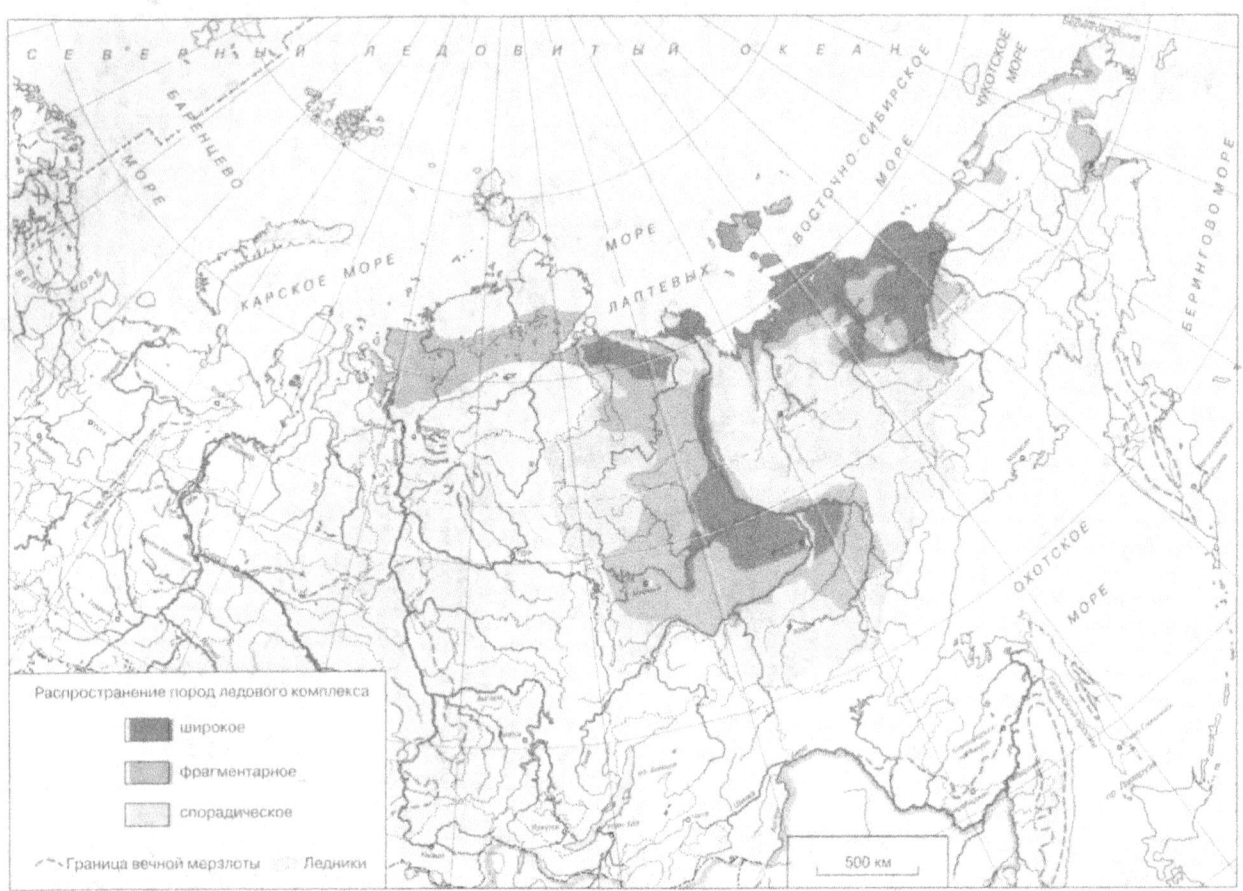

Figure 3.   Map showing Yedoma distribution, Siberia, Russia, by Konishchev (2011) with three distinct types of Yedoma distribution: Dark blue, widely distributed; Medium blue, fragmented; Light blue, sporadic. Red dashed line is boundary of permafrost. White dotted areas are glaciers.

Data and Methods

Quaternary Geological Maps

We acquired 11 digital copies of Russian Quaternary geological maps at a scale of 1:1,000,000 for the core region of known Yedoma distribution in central and eastern Siberia (fig. 4).The original paper maps were issued by the Department of Natural Resources of the Russian Federation or its predecessor, the Department of Geology of the Soviet Union. All maps are part of the "New Series", produced as an update to the "First Series".

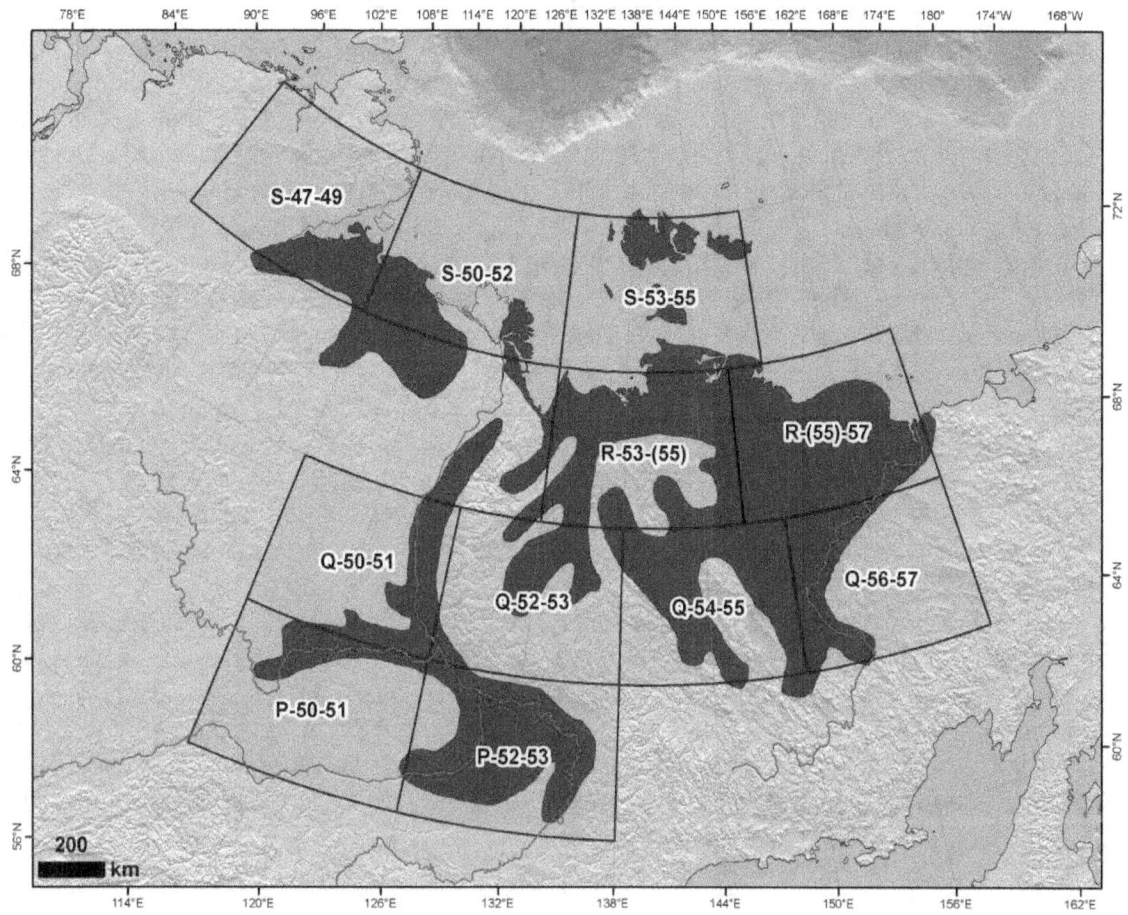

Figure 4. Map showing location of the 11 Quaternary geological maps at a scale of 1:1,000,000 that were included in the Yedoma database, Siberia, Russia, as of 2013. Red polygons indicate the Yedoma core region after Romanovskii (1993) (fig. 2). References for each Quaternary map are provided in appendix A.

9

The maps are the product of decades of geological field and remote sensing work and mapping at scales of 1:50,000–1:500,000 by Russian geologists and cartographers in the respective regions. A complete list of map references is provided in appendix A. The 11 maps encompass a total area of 2,785,000 km^2, of which 2,324,500 km^{2}are onshore land area. The maps generally contain information on lithofacies type, lithology, and stratigraphy for each unit. Each polygon of a geological unit in the map has a Unit ID (for example, LIII$_{2-4}$) and color assigned that indicate a certain lithofacies and stratigraphy (fig. 5). On each map, either a map legend or a table cross-tabulating lithofacies type with stratigraphy provides a short description of the unit. An additional pattern signature in the polygon of a certain map unit usually represents lithology, and this information is provided in a separate legend. Each map also has one or several geological cross profiles that are to scale horizontally, but are exaggerated or not to scale vertically. Here, the same colors, signatures, and unit IDs are used as in the map (fig. 5). Additionally, signatures here indicate the presence of large ice wedges in a unit. The stratigraphic schemes applied by the original map authors in these 11 maps varied by map tile, likely owing to regional differences, and the long time frame during which these maps were published (1981–2000, see publication dates in appendix A) and related changes in stratigraphic naming conventions. In particular, the use of different terms for the late Pleistocene stratigraphic horizons even in adjacent map tiles initially may be confusing. For guidance, we provide a table comparing the different stratigraphic schemes of the late Pleistocene used in these 11 maps and link them to schemes used in other regions as well as marine isotope stages (MIS) (appendix B).

Rectification of all maps was conducted in ArcGIS 9.3™ and ArcGIS 10.0™ desktop geographic information system (GIS) software from Environmental Systems Research Institute, Inc. (ESRI). All maps were georeferenced to a Gauss-Krueger projection, known in the U.S. as Transverse Mercator projection, with geodetic datum Pulkovo 1942 using the latitude-longitude grid provided in the maps. Appendix C provides details on number of control points used for the rectification, the Root Mean Square (RMS) error from a 3rd polynomial transformation, and the Gauss-Kruger zone of the target projection that differs for each map tile. RMS errors range from 130 to 300 m, which is a reasonable range for this map scale.

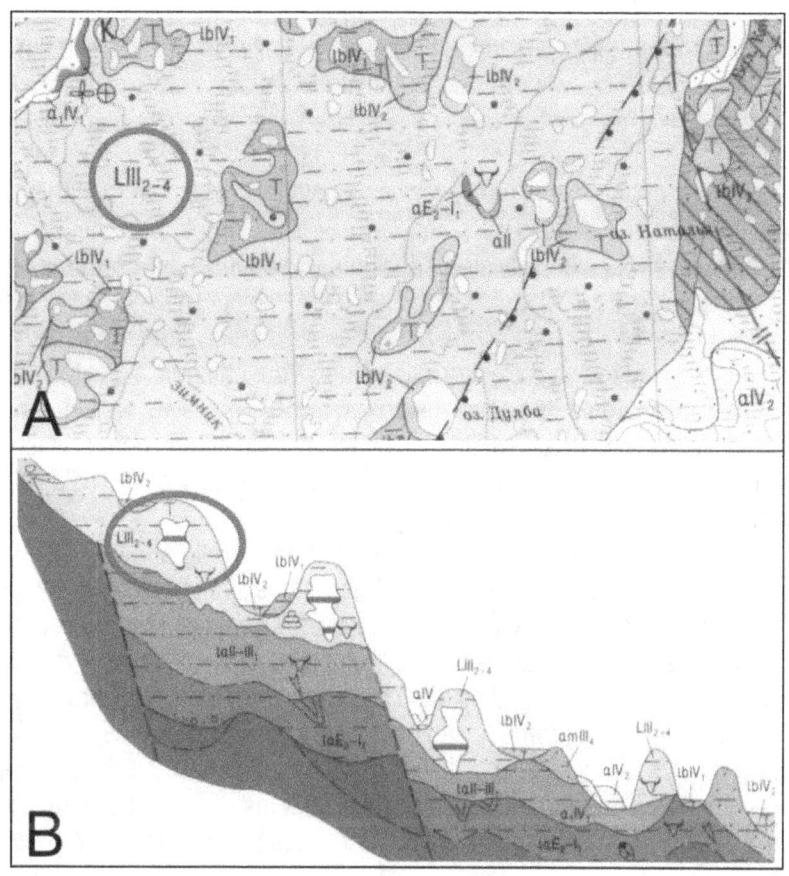

Figure 5. Example of geological unit in map R-(55)-57 that is interpreted as Yedoma, Siberia, Russia. A, Map view: Orange-colored unit LIII$_{2-4}$ (label circled in red) is described in the legend as loess (L) of Late Pleistocene stratigraphy (III), specifically covering the periods Zyryan, Kargin, and Sartan (2–4). The lithologic signatures (dash-dot-dash) identify this unit as deposits with mostly silty to fine-sandy grain size, and the dark blue dots indicate very high ground ice contents. Abundance of lakes (light blue) and lacustrine deposits (medium and dark blue, lbIV$_1$ and lbIV$_2$) within the unit indicate degradation of at least the upper part of the Yedoma unit by Holocene thermokarst. B, Cross-profile view: The same unit LIII$_{2-4}$ (red circle) is shown to blanket terrace slopes. Animal skull symbol indicates presence of fossil bones of the mammoth fauna. White features with blue stripes indicate presence of very large syngenetic ice wedges typical for Yedoma.

Digitizing the Yedoma Polygons

The 11 georeferenced maps were loaded into ArcGIS software for digitizing the polygons containing Yedoma deposits. Each digital map was processed to extract geologic contacts (black-colored borders of geologic map units) from the rest of the map. The ArcScan tool in ArcGIS was used to automatically trace each raster contact into a vector line to allow snapping to the contact center line during digitization. These lines were edited on screen to remove text, map patterns, and the occasional contour lines that were automatically converted to lines. Dangling lines were removed and all lines were checked to ensure proper polygon topology. Once the lines were created, a point feature class was manually created to contain attribution for polygons. The line and point feature classes were used in the Feature to Polygon tool to create the geologic polygons. Polygons containing Yedoma deposits were extracted from the geologic map feature class into a polygon feature class containing only Yedoma deposits. Theses feature classes were projected into a North Pole Lambert Azimuthal Equal Area projection to maintain consistent area measurements across the entire region. The newly projected polygon feature classes then were merged into a single feature class. We maintained all attribute information for each individual polygon from its original Russian source map, geologic unit, and quadrangle map name. We also calculated area in square kilometers and perimeter in kilometers for each polygon.

We selected the Yedoma polygons based on their narrow stratigraphy (usually late Pleistocene QIII$_{2-4}$), their loessic, loessic-cryogenic, or sometimes alluvial or lacustrine lithofacies type, and an additional pattern signature indicating very ice-rich ground (fig. 5). Additionally, the geologic cross sections indicate the presence of large syngenetic ice wedges with not-to-scale wedge-like shapes in these units. Furthermore, our first-hand field knowledge from various Siberian Yedoma sites and knowledge from scientific literature guided our decision on which units should be attributed to Yedoma based on spatial location and association. A complete list of units included in the Yedoma polygons in each map tile is provided in appendix D. We also were careful to remove inconsistencies between the different maps caused by the Yedoma deposits being mapped as different geologic units by different map authors and some naming inconsistencies between maps resulting in identical units being named differently.

Preliminary Results

A total area of 290,101 km^2 of Yedoma is identified for the 11 maps contained in our database (table 3). A preliminary analysis of this refined map of Yedoma distribution in the core regions of its occurrence suggests that the total panarctic extent of Yedoma may be substantially smaller than previously assumed based on estimates derived from small-scale maps (compare fig. 6 with fig. 4). For the same map tiles, we estimated a Yedoma cover of 1,028,264 km^2 based on the Romanovskii (1993) small-scale map. Therefore, our updated coverage represents a total decrease of 71.8 percent from the original estimate for these areas. Yedoma is most extensive in the Yana-Indigirka-Kolyma lowlands, the New Siberian Islands, and the central Yakutian lowlands east of the Lena River. However, even here, Yedoma only covers as much as 35.7 percent of the land area based on the Quaternary geological maps (fig. 6). Because Yedoma is known to occur primarily in lowlands and foothills, we separately estimated the ratio of Yedoma cover for the total area of individual maps as well as for lowland and foothill areas within the 0–400 m elevation range for individual maps. For such lowlands and foothills, Yedoma cover in the 11 map tiles ranges from 1.1 to 35.8 percent and averages 16.9 percent for the studied region, according to our database. The distribution of Yedoma units shows an often substantial spatial discontinuity of these ice-rich deposits because of strong dissection by thermokarst and thermal and fluvial erosion, highlighting the important role of these processes for transforming the late Pleistocene accumulation plain through erosion and permafrost degradation during the Holocene. Previous estimates of the amount of soil organic carbon stored in Yedoma must be revised downwards based on the lower total coverage we found in this study compared to the previously assumed 1 million square kilometer Yedoma coverage. A full analysis should include spatial data from all Yedoma regions as well as substantial field data on ground ice distribution, soil organic carbon distribution and characteristics, bulk densities, and thickness of Yedoma deposits.

Table 3. Identified total Yedoma areas, Siberia, Russia, in each map tile in the database. Lowlands were defined as landareas with elevations of 0–400m above mean sea level as derived from a digital elevation model with 90-m spatial resolution.

Map tile	Total map area [km²]	Total land area [km²]	Total lowland area <400m [km²]	Yedoma cover [km²]		Ratio of Yedoma vs. land area [%]		Reduction over old Yedoma area estimate [%]	Ratio of Yedoma vs. lowland area [%]
				Old*	New**	Old*	New**		New**
P-50-51	280,238	280,238	248,832	37,442	2,734	13.4	1.0	-92.7	1.1
P-52-53	280,238	280,238	220,853	149,358	41,237	53.3	14.7	-72.4	18.7
Q-50-51	242,970	242,970	236,109	60,261	17,287	24.8	7.1	-71.3	7.3
Q-52-53	242,970	242,970	42,406	60,165	1,526	24.8	0.6	-97.5	3.6
Q-54-55	242,970	242,970	65,038	139,860	6,214	57.6	2.6	-95.6	9.6
Q-56-57	242,970	242,970	167,649	74,226	35,612	30.5	14.7	-52.0	21.2
R-53-(55)	255,555	240,349	197,379	164,171	52,541	68.3	21.9	-68.0	26.6
R-(55)- 57	255,555	196,235	195,706	190,552	70,016	97.1	35.7	-63.3	35.8
S-47-49	247,281	226,620	214,013	47,113	35,082	20.8	15.5	-25.5	16.4
S-50-52	247,281	74,626	74,601	50,748	13,464	68.0	18.0	-73.5	18.0
S-53-55	247,281	54,367	54,361	54,367	14,387	100.0	26.5	-73.5	26.5
Total	**2,785,309**	**2,324,553**	**1,716,946**	**1,028,264**	**290,101**	**44.2**	**12.5**	**-71.8**	**16.9**

* Based on Yedoma map from Romanovskii (1993), as used in Zimov and others (2006a, 2006b).
** This study

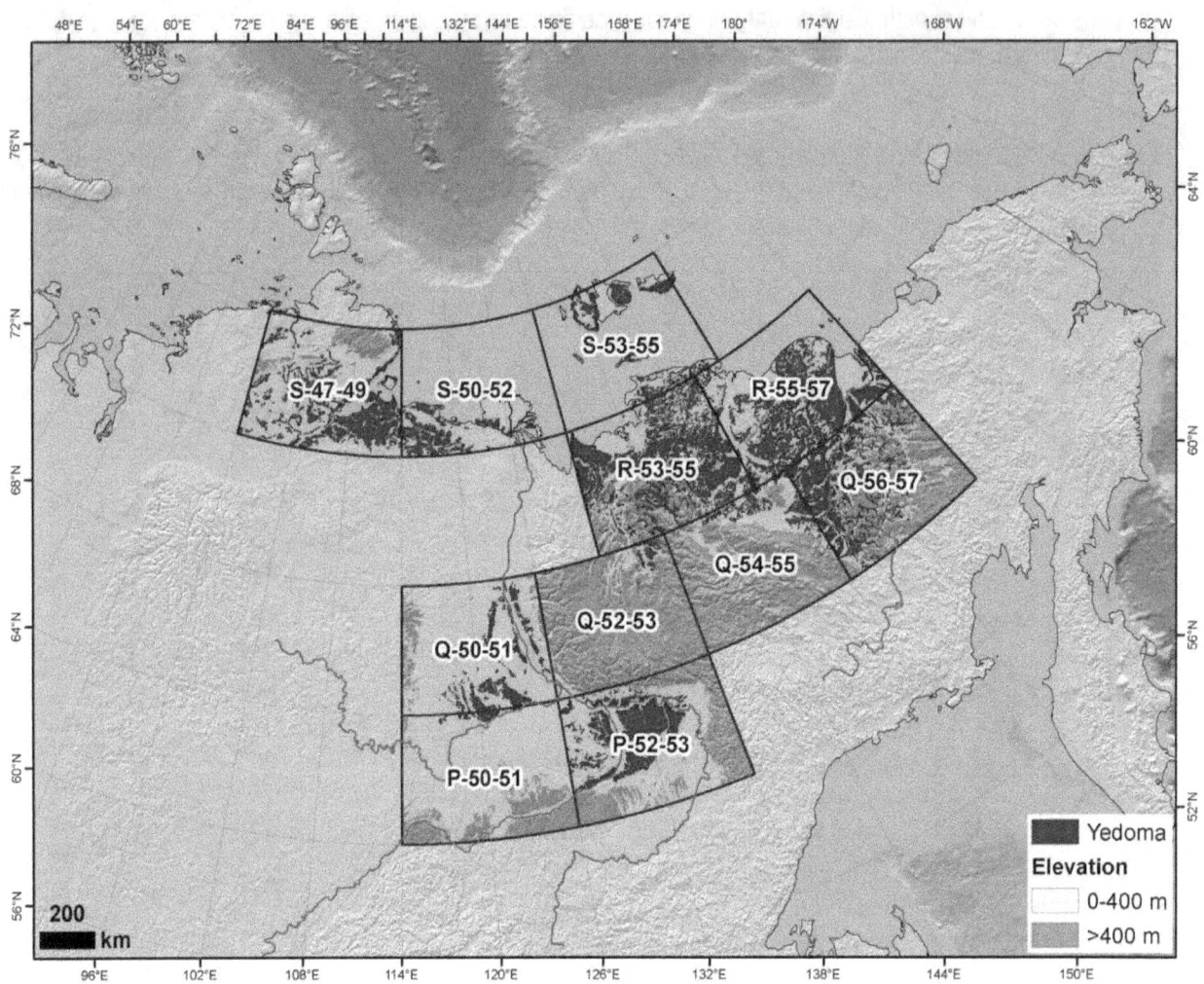

Figure 6. Map showing updated Yedoma coverage, Siberia, Russia, for each map tile in the database. In addition, lowlands and uplands are indicated, demonstrating that Yedoma is restricted mainly to elevations between 0–400 meters above mean sea level.

Product Limitations and Future Updates

The new Yedoma geospatial database (version 1.0) greatly reduces uncertainties in Yedoma distribution for the region covered by the 11 included map tiles. Previous Yedoma area estimates were based on maps at a scale of 1:10,000,000 or smaller, which generalized the distribution of Yedoma. Such small-scale maps actually show the potential Yedoma presence in a region rather than the spatially explicit distribution. However, the medium-scale maps (scale 1:1,000,000) used here also have some limitations. Although they can better capture the spatial heterogeneity and discontinuity of Yedoma extent, they still may misrepresent Yedoma absence or presence at a particular location owing to necessary map generalization (1 cm in the map = 10 km in reality).

General accuracy of the Yedoma distribution shown in this database is tied to several potential error sources: (1) uncertainties in the original geologic and cryostratigraphic mapping, (2) uncertainties in converting and scaling the original field and remote sensing data to a paper map product, (3) uncertainties in the technical conversion from a paper map to a digital geodatabase, and (4) uncertainties in interpretation of Quaternary geological units across multiple map tiles as a Yedoma unit. We had no control over uncertainties in (1) and (2) because we used each map as-is and assumed that the quality control of the original Russian geologic, stratigraphic, and cartographic work was rigorous. In (3), mostly geometric uncertainties are included, such as the accuracy of georeferencing the maps (appendix B), and the line thickness of geologic boundaries and their digitization accuracy. Geologic boundaries drawn as black lines in these maps frequently have a real-world footprint of 100–200 m in width and, therefore, location accuracy of digitized lines are within the RMS error range of the map rectification. The accuracy of digital polygons of geologic units in each map (both location and geologic unit association) was cross-checked against the source map by several members of the project team, and, if necessary, was corrected. To limit errors in (4), we relied on existing scientific literature and our field knowledge of Siberian Yedoma. In most cases, the maps provide evidence that a certain unit is ice-rich, syngenetic, late Pleistocene Yedoma by that unit's cryolithofacies and stratigraphic signatures in the plan map view and the geologic crossprofiles. In few cases, no signature for high ground-ice content or syngenetic ice wedges was included in the map. However, it was possible to trace such units by comparing them with neighboring polygons in directly adjacent map tiles and inferring that they are the same units if spatially connected.

An additional need to carefully evaluate the Yedoma database arises from the fact that a two-dimensional surface geological map cannot properly represent the total spatial extent of geologic horizons that potentially overlap in three dimensions. The Yedoma units represented in the maps and the database are likely those that crop out close to the land surface and that probably have a certain minimum thickness. The geological crossprofile in figure 5B is an example of where Yedoma is overlain by Holocene lacustrine and alluvial deposits, suggesting the possibility that some Yedoma is covered by other, younger geological units. Although thermokarst lake deposits in many cases indicate that the entire underlying Yedoma has thawed out, shallow lakes may not have fully degraded Yedoma underneath. Similarly, younger eolian or alluvial deposits may cover late Pleistocene Yedoma units. Therefore, it is unclear whether any Yedoma remains beneath the lacustrine and alluvial sediments shown in figure 5A. Such geological situations would make the identified extent of Yedoma in the database a conservative low estimate that needs to be corroborated with additional evidence.

Yedoma occurs in other regions not yet covered by our database, such as in the lowlands south of the Taymyr Peninsula and various regions in Chukotka (figs. 2 and 3). The ultimate goal would be to create a circumarctic database that, in addition to including a complete Siberian Yedoma extent, also includes data from maps of similar or finer scale for Yedoma deposits in Alaska and northwestern Canada. The Yedoma spatial database would be linked to the Northern Circumpolar Soil Carbon Database (NCSCD) (Hugelius and others, 2013). In addition to expanding the Yedoma database, a next step should include the full digitization of all geologic map units, which would provide useful information for a range of analyses including the quantification of soil organic carbon pools in a variety of near-surface permafrost deposits. Schirrmeister and others (2011) have shown for the Laptev Sea region in northern Siberia that different stratigraphic horizons naturally have different soil carbon stocks and characteristics. This has implications for overall deep soil carbon storage as well as the vulnerability, pathways, and impacts of carbon mobilization in permafrost regions. Similarly, Harden and others (2012) have shown that the vertical distribution of deep soil organic carbon in various permafrost soil orders differs and has implications for potential mobilization.

Conclusions

Yedoma deposits quantified for a 2,324,500 square kilometers land area in central and eastern Siberia cover about 290,101 square kilometers, representing about 12.5 percent of the land area and 16.9 percent of the lowlands below 400 meters in elevation. These findings suggest a substantial reduction of previous estimates of Yedoma coverage (1,000,000 square kilometers). Yedoma areas are highly fragmented in northern Siberia at map scales of 1:1,000,000. Spatial fragmentation of this late Pleistocene cover deposit is mainly a result of Holocene thermokarst processes and fluvial erosion. Therefore, when quantifying the deep soil carbon pools in the Yedoma permafrost region of Siberia, it is of critical importance to exclude thermokarst and fluvial deposits from the Yedoma class and to address carbon pools separately for a more complete assessment. Deep and frozen soil carbon pools in the vast Siberian Yedoma region remain understudied, and not much is known about their vulnerability and feedback in a changing climate.

Disclaimer

All data in the Yedoma geospatial database (v.1.0) is provided as is and should not be used at map scales finer than 1:1,000,000. Original Russian map data were not altered except for the purpose of selecting geological units that are interpreted as Yedoma and merging these units across map tiles into a single data layer for analysis.

Acknowledgments

We thank the U.S. Geological Survey and the Alfred Wegener Institute for Polar and Marine Research, Potsdam, Germany, for support of this digital data compilation. We are very thankful for valuable support from the Los Altos Hills Foothill College GeoSpatial Technology Certificate Program in Geographic Information Sciences, and, specifically, from K. Allison Lenkeit Meexan for recruiting well-trained volunteers. Funding was provided through USGS, NSF OPP 0732735, and NASA NNX08AJ37G. We thank G. Hugelius and D. Swanson for their helpful reviews and the editors of the USGS for their helpful technical review.

References Cited

Andreev, A.A., Grosse, G., Schirrmeister, L., Kuznetsova, T.V., Kuzmina, S.A., Bobrov, A.A., Tarasov, P.E., Novenko, E.Y., Meyer, H., Derevyagin, A.Y., Kienast, F., Bryantseva, A., and Kunitsky, V.V., 2009, Weichselian and Holocene palaeoenvironmental history of the Bol'shoy Lyakhovsky Island, New Siberian Archipelago, Arctic Siberia: Boreas, v. 38, p. 72–110.

Carter, L.D., 1988, Loess and deep thermokarst basins in Arctic Alaska: Tapir Publishers, Trondheim, Norway, 5th International Conference on Permafrost, August 2–5, 1988, p. 706–711.

Froese, D.G., Zazula, G.D., Westgate, J.A., Preece, S.J., Sanborn, P.T., Reyes, A.V., and Pearce, N.J.G., 2009, The Klondike goldfields and Pleistocene environments of Beringia: Geological Society of America (GSA) Today, v. 19, p. 4–10.

Galabala, R.O., 1997, Pereletki and the initiation of glaciation in Siberia: Quaternary International, v. 41–42, p. 27–32.

Gravis, G.F., 1969, Fossil slope deposits in the northern Arctic asymmetrical valleys: Biuletyn Peryglacjalny, v. 20, p. 239–257.

Gravis, G.F., 1997, Role of fluvial processes in evolution of ice complex soils: Kriosfera Zemli, v. 1, no. 2, p. 56–59. [In Russian.]

Grigoriev, M.N., and Kunitsky, V.V., 2000, Ice complex of the Arctic coasts of Yakutia as a sediment source on the continental shelf, *in* Hydrometeorological and biogeochemical research in the Arctic region: Vladivostok, Russia, Dalnauka Press, Arctic Regional Centre, v. 2, p. 109–116. [In Russian.]

Grosse, G., Harden, J., Turetsky, M., McGuire, A.D., Camill, P., Tarnocai, C., Frolking, S., Schuur, E.A.G., Jorgenson, T., Marchenko, S., Romanovsky, V., Wickland, K.P., French, N., Waldrop, M., Bourgeau-Chavez, L., and Striegl, R.G., 2011, Vulnerability of high-latitude soil organic carbon in North America to disturbance: Journal of Geophysical Research, v. 116, G00K06, 23 p.

Grosse, G., Schirrmeister, L., and Malthus, T., 2006, Application of Landsat-7 satellite data and a DEM for the quantification of thermokarst-affected terrain types in the periglacial Lena–Anabar coastal lowland: Polar Research, v. 25, no. 1, p. 51–67.

Grosse, G., Schirrmeister, L., Siegert, C., Kunitsky, V.V., Slagoda, E.A., Andreev, A.A., and Dereviagyn, A.Y., 2007, Geological and geomorphological evolution of a sedimentary periglacial landscape in northeast Siberia during the Late Quaternary: Geomorphology, v. 86, no. 1–2, p. 25–51.

Grosswald, M.G., 1998, Late-Weichselian ice sheets in Arctic and Pacific Siberia: Quaternary International, v. 45-46, p. 3–18.

Gusev, A.I., 1958, On the stratigraphy of Quaternary deposits of the western part of the coastal plain: Sbornik statey po geologii Arktiki, Trudy NIIGA, v. 5, p. 79–86. [In Russian.]

Hamilton, T.D., Craig, J.L., and Sellmann, P.V., 1988, The Fox permafrost tunnel—A late Quaternary geologic record in central Alaska: Geological Society of America Bulletin, v. 100, no. 6, p. 948–969.

Harden, J.W., Koven, C.D., Ping, C.-L., Hugelius, G., McGuire, A.D., Camill, P., Jorgenson, M.T., Kuhry, P., Michaelson, G.J., O'Donnell, J.A., Schuur, E.A.G., Tarnocai, C., Johnson, K., and Grosse, G., 2012, Field information links permafrost carbon to physical vulnerabilities of thawing: Geophysical Research Letters, v. 39, L15704, 6 p.

Hubberten, H.W., Andreev, A., Astakhov, V.I., Demidov, I., Dowdeswell, J.A., Henriksen, M., Hjort, C., Houmark-Nielsen, M., Jakobsson, M., Kuzmina, S., Larsen, E., Lunkka, J.P., Lysa, A., Mangerud, J., Moller, P., Saarnisto, M., Schirrmeister, L., Sher, A.V., Siegert, C., Siegert, M.J., and Svendsen, J.I., 2004, The periglacial climate and environment in northern Eurasia during the last glaciation: Quaternary Science Reviews, v. 23, no. 11–13, p. 1333–1357.

Hugelius, G., Tarnocai, C., Broll, G., Canadell, J. G., Kuhry, P., and Swanson, D. K., 2013, The Northern Circumpolar Soil Carbon Database—Spatially distributed datasets of soil coverage and soil carbon storage in the northern permafrost regions: Earth System Sciences Data, v. 5, p. 3–13.

Ivanov, O.A., 1972, Stratigraphy and correlation of Neogene and Quaternary deposits in the subarctic plains of East Yakutia—Problems of Quaternary period research: Moscow, Nauka Press, p. 202–21 1. [In Russian.]

Kanevskiy, M., Shur, Y., Fortier, D., Jorgenson, M.T. and Stephani, E., 2011, Cryostratigraphy of late Pleistocene syngenetic permafrost (Yedoma) in northern Alaska, Itkillik River exposure: Quaternary Research, v. 75, no. 3, p. 584–596.

Kaplina, T.N., 1981, History of permafrost in Northern Yakutia during the late Cenozoic, History of the development of perennial frozen deposits in Eurasia: Moscow, Nauka Press, p. 153–181. [In Russian.]

Katasonov, E.M., 1975, Frozen ground and facial analysis of Pleistocene deposits and paleogeography of Central Yakutia: Biuletyn Peryglacjalny, v. 24, p. 33–41.

Kayalaynen, E.M., and Kulakov, Y.N., 1966, On the question of paleogeography of the Yana-Indigirka (Coastal) Lowland during the Neogene-Quaternary time, in Saks, V.N., ed., Chetvertichnyy period Sibiri: Moscow, Nauka Press, p. 274–282. [In Russian.]

Kienel, U., Siegert, C., and Hahne, J., 1999, Late Quaternary palaeoenvironmental reconstructions from a permafrost sequence (North Siberian Lowland, SE Taymyr Peninsula)—A multidisciplinary case study: Boreas, v. 28, p. 181–193.

Konishchev, V.N., 1981, Formation of fine-grained ground in the cryolithosphere: Novosibirsk, Russia, Nauka Press, 197 p. [In Russian.]

Konishchev, V.N., 1987, Origin of loess-like silt in Northern Jakutia, USSR: GeoJournal, v. 15., no. 2, p. 135–139.

Konishchev, V.N., 2011, Permafrost response to climate warming: Kriosfera Zemli, v. 4, p. 15–18. [In Russian.]

Konishchev, V.N., and Rogov, V.V., 1993, Investigations of cryogenic weathering in Europe and Northern Asia: Permafrost and Periglacial Processes, v. 4, p. 49–64.

Kotler, E., and Burn, C.R., 2000, Cryostratigraphy of the Klondike "muck" deposits, west-central Yukon Territory: Canadian Journal of Earth Sciences, v. 37, p. 849–861.

Kuhry, P., Dorrepaal, E., Hugelius, G., Schuur, E.A.G., and Tarnocai, C., 2010, Potential remobilization of belowground permafrost carbon under future global warming: Permafrost and Periglacial Processes, v. 21, no. 2, p. 208-214.

Kunitsky, V.V., 1989, Cryolithogenesis of the lower Lena [Kriolitologiya nizo'ev Leny]: Yakutsk, Russia, Permafrost Institute Press, 162 p. [In Russian].

Kunitsky, V.V., 2007, Nival lithogenesis and Ice Complex on the territory of Yakutia [Nivalnuy litogenesi Ledovuy Kompleks na territorii Yakutii]: Yakutsk, Russia, Permafrost Institute, Russian Academy of Sciences Siberian Section, Extended abstract of doctoral dissertation, 46 p. [In Russian.]

Kunitsky, V.V., Schirrmeister, L., Grosse, G., and Kienast, F., 2002, Snow patches in nival landscapes and their role for the Ice Complex formation in the Laptev Sea coastal lowlands: Polarforschung v. 70, p. 53–67.

Lavrushin, Y.A., 1962, Stratigraphy and some peculiarities of Quaternary deposits formation in the lower reaches of the Indigirka River: Izvestiya Akademii Nauk SSSR, Seriya Geologicheskaya, v. 2, p. 73–87. [in Russian.]

McGuire, A.D., Macdonald, R.W., Schuur, E.A.G., Harden, J.W., Kuhry, P., Hayes, D.J., Christensen, T.R., and Heimann, M., 2010, The carbon budget of the northern cryosphere region: Current Opinion in Environmental Sustainability, v. 2, no. 4, p. 231–236.

Meyer, H., Derevyagin, A.Y., Siegert, C., and Hubberten, H.-W., 2002a, Paleoclimate studies on Bykovsky Peninsula, north Siberia—Hydrogen and oxygen isotopes in ground ice: Polarforschung, v. 70, p. 37–51.

Meyer, H., Dereviagin, A., Siegert, C., Schirrmeister, L., and Hubberten, H.-W., 2002b, Palaeoclimate reconstruction on Big Lyakhovsky Island, north Siberia—Hydrogen and oxygen isotopes in ice wedges: Permafrost and Periglacial Processes, v. 13, p. 91–105.

Nagaoka, D., 1994, Properties of Ice Complex deposits in eastern Siberia, in Inoue, G., ed., Proceedings of the Second Symposium on the Joint Siberian Permafrost Studies between Japan and Russia in 1993, Tsukuba, Japan, p. 14–18.

Péwé, T.L., 1955, Origin of the upland silt near Fairbanks, Alaska: Geological Society of America (GSA) Bulletin, v. 66, no. 6, p. 699–724.

Péwé, T.L., 1975, Quaternary geology of Alaska: U.S. Geological Survey Professional Paper, v. 835, 145 p.

Péwé, T.L., and Journaux, A., 1983, Origin and character of loess-like silt in unglaciated south-central Yakutia, Siberia, U.S.S.R.: U. S. Geological Survey Professional Paper 1262, 46 p.

Péwé, T.L., Journaux, A., and Stuckenrath, R., 1977, Radiocarbon dates and late-Quaternary stratigraphy from Mamontova Gora, unglaciated central Yakutia, Siberia, U.S.S.R: Quaternary Research, v. 8, no. 1, p. 51–63.

Popov, A.I., 1953, Features of lithogenesis of alluvial plains under the conditions of cold climate: Izvestiya AN SSSR, Seriya Geograficheskaya, v. 2, p. 29–41. [In Russian.]

Popov, A.I., 1969, Underground ice in the Quaternary deposits of the Yana-Indigirka lowland as a genetic and stratigraphic indicator, in Péwé, T.L., ed., The periglacial environment, past and present: Montreal, Canada, Arctic Institute of North America, p. 55–64.

Romanovskii, N.N., 1958, Paleogeographic conditions of formation of the Quaternary deposits on Bol'shoy Lyakhovsky Island (New Siberian Islands), in Bogorov, V.G., ed., Questions of physical geography of Polar region: Moscow, Publications of Moscow State University, p. 80–88. [In Russian.]

Romanovskii, N.N., 1977, Formation of polygonal ice wedge structures [Formirovanie poligonal'no-zhil'nikh struktur]: Novosibirsk, Russia, Nauka Press. [In Russian.]

Romanovskii, N.N., 1993, Principles of cryogenesis in the lithosphere [Osnovy Kriogeneza Litosfery]: Moscow, Moscow State University Press, 335 p. [In Russian.]

Sanborn, P.T., Smith, C.A.S., Froese, D.G., Zazula, G.D., and Westgate, J.A., 2006, Full-glacial paleosols in perennially frozen loess sequences, Klondike goldfields, Yukon Territory, Canada: Quaternary Research, v. 66, p. 147–157.

Schirrmeister, L., Froese, D., Tumskoy, V., Grosse, G., and Wetterich, S., 2013, Yedoma—Late Pleistocene ice-rich syngenetic permafrost of Beringia, *in* Elias, S.A., ed., The Encyclopedia of Quaternary Science, Amsterdam, The Netherlands, Elsevier, v. 3, p. 542-552.

Schirrmeister, L., Grosse, G., Kunitsky, V., Magens, D., Meyer, H., Dereviagin, A., Kuznetsova, T., Andreev, A., Babiy, O., Kienast, F., Grigoriev, M., Overduin, P.P., and Preusser, F., 2008, Periglacial landscape evolution and environmental changes of Arctic lowland areas for the last 60,000 years (western Laptev Sea coast, Cape Mamontov Klyk): Polar Research, v. 27, p. 249–272.

Schirrmeister, L., Grosse, G., Schwamborn, G., Andreev, A.A., Meyer, H., Kunitsky, V.V., Kuznetsova, T.V., Dorozhkina, M.V., Pavlova, E.Y., Bobrov, A.A., and Oezen, D., 2003, Late Quaternary History of the Accumulation Plain North of the Chekanovsky Ridge (Lena Delta, Russia): A Multidisciplinary Approach: Polar Geography, v. 27, p. 277–319.

Schirrmeister, L., Grosse, G., Wetterich, S., Overduin, P.P., Strauss, J., Schuur, E.A.G., and Hubberten, H.-W., 2011a, Fossil organic matter characteristics in permafrost deposits of the northeast Siberian Arctic: Journal of Geophysical Research, v. 116, G00M02, 16 p.

Schirrmeister, L., Kunitsky, V., Grosse, G., Wetterich, S., Meyer, H., Schwamborn, G., Babiy, O., Derevyagin, A., and Siegert, C., 2011b, Sedimentary characteristics and origin of the late Pleistocene Ice Complex on north-east Siberian Arctic coastal lowlands and islands—A review: Quaternary International, v. 241, p. 3–25.

Schirrmeister, L., Siegert, C., Kunitsky, V.V., Grootes, P.M., and Erlenkeuser, H., 2001, Late Quaternary ice-rich permafrost sequences as a paleoenvironmental archive for the Laptev Sea region in northern Siberia: International Journal of Earth Sciences, v. 91, p. 154–167.

Schirrmeister, L., Siegert, C., Kuznetsova, T., Kuzmina, S., Andreev, A., Kienast, F., Meyer, H., and Bobrov, A., 2002, Paleoenvironmental and paleoclimatic records from permafrost deposits in the Arctic region of northern Siberia: Quaternary International, v. 89, p. 97–118.

Schuur, E.A.G., Bockheim, J., Canadell, J.G., Euskirchen, E., Field, C.B., Goryachkin, S.V., Hagemann, S., Kuhry, P., Lafleur, P.M., Lee, H., Mazhitova, G., Nelson, F.E., Rinke, A., Romanovsky, V.E., Shiklomanov, N., Tarnocai, C., Venevsky, S., Vogel, J.G., and Zimov, S.A., 2008. Vulnerability of permafrost carbon to climate change—Implications for the global carbon cycle. BioScience, v. 58, no. 8, p. 701–714.

Sher, A.V., 1995, Is there any real evidence for a huge shelf ice sheet in east Siberia?: Quaternary International, v. 28, p. 39–40.

Sher, A.V., 1997, Yedoma as a store of paleoenvironmental records in Beringida: Beringian Paleoenvironments Workshop, Florissant, Colorado, September 20–23, 1997, Program and Abstracts, p. 140–144.

Sher, A.V., Kaplina, T.N., and Ovander, M.G., 1987, Unified regional stratigraphic chart for the Quaternary deposits in the Yana-Kolyma lowland and its mountainous surroundings—Explanatory note, *in* Decisions of Interdepartmental Stratigraphic Conference on the Quaternary of the East USSR: Magadan, Russia, USSR Academy of Sciences, Far-Eastern Branch, North-Eastern Complex Research Institute, p.29–60. [In Russian.]

Sher, A.V., Kuzmina, S.A., Kuznetsova, T.V., and Sulerzhitsky, L.D., 2005, New insights into the Weichselian environment and climate of the east Siberian Arctic, derived from fossil insects, plants, and mammals: Quaternary Science Reviews v. 24, p. 533–569.

Shur, Y., French, H.M., Bray, M.T., and Anderson, D.A., 2004, Syngenetic permafrost growth—Cryostratigraphic observations from the CRREL tunnel near Fairbanks, Alaska: Permafrost and Periglacial Processes, v. 15, p. 339–347.

Siegert, C., and Romanovskii, N.N., 1996, The late Pleistocene "Ice Complex"—A Phenomenon of the non-glaciated areas of northern Eurasia: Quaternary Environment of the Eurasian North (QUEEN)—Proceedings of the 1st Annual Workshop, Strasbourg, France, November 29–December 2, 1996.

Siegert, C., Schirrmeister, L., Kunitsky, V.V., Meyer, H., Kuznetsova, T., Dereviagyn, A.,Kuzmina, S., Tumskoy, V., and Sher, A., 1999, Paleoclimate signals of ice-rich permafrost: Alfred Wegener Institute (AWI) Reports on Polar and Marine Research, v. 315, p. 145–259.

Siegert, C., Schirrmeister, L., and Babiy, O.A., 2000, The sedimentological, mineralogical, and geochemical composition of late Pleistocene permafrost deposits from the Ice Complex on the Bykovsky Peninsula, northern Siberia: Polarforschung, v. 70, p. 3–11.

Slagoda, E.A., 1991, Microstructure features of the deposits of Ice Complexes in northern Yakutia (by the example of Bykovsky Peninsula), in Gilichinsky, D.A., ed., Kriologiya pochv: Pushchino, Russia, IPFS PNTs AN SSR, p. 38–47. [In Russian.]

Slagoda, E.A., 1993, Genesis and microstructure of cryolithogenic deposits at the Bykovsky Peninsula and the Muostakh Island: Yakutsk, Russia, Permafrost Institute, Russian Academy of Sciences Siberian Section, dissertation thesis, 218 p. [In Russian.]

Strauss, J., Schirrmeister, L., Wetterich, S., Borchers, A., and Davydov, S.P., 2012, Grain-size properties and organic-carbon stock of Yedoma Ice Complex permafrost from the Kolyma lowland, northeastern Siberia: Global Biogeochemical Cycles, v. 26, GB3003, 12 p.

Streletskaya, I.D., Gusev, E.A., Visiliev, A.A., Kanevskiy, M., Anikina, N., and Derevyanko, L., 2007, New results from complex investigations on Quaternary deposits of western Taymyr: Kriosfera Zemli, v. 3, p. 14–28. [In Russian.]

Strelkov, S.A., 1960, Stratigraphy of Quaternary deposits of the Laptev and western part of theEast-Siberian Sea coasts: Magadan, Russia, Trudy Mezhved. soveshch., stratigr. Skhema Sev.-Vost. SSSR, p. 468–471. [In Russian.]

Taber, S., 1958, Complex origin of silts in the vicinity of Fairbanks, Alaska: Geological Society of America (GSA) Bulletin, v. 69, p. 131–136.

Tarnocai, C., Canadell, J.G., Schuur, E.A.G., Kuhry, P., Mazhitova, G., and Zimov, S., 2009, Soil organic carbon pools in the northern circumpolar permafrost region: Global Biogeochemical Cycles, v. 23, GB2023, 11 p.

Tomirdiaro, S.V., 1980, Loess-ice formations in east Siberia during the late Pleistocene and Holocene: Moscow, Nauka Press, 184 p. [In Russian.]

Tomirdiaro, S.V., Arslanov, Kh.A.,Chernen'kiy, B.I., Tertychnaya, T.V., and Prokhorova, T.N., 1984, New data on the formation of loess-ice sequences in northern Yakutia and ecological conditions of the mammoth fauna in the Arctic during the late Pleistocene: Doklady Akademiy Nauk SSSR, v. 278, no. 6, p. 1446–1449. [In Russian.]

Tomirdiaro, S.V., and Chernen'kiy, B.I., 1987, Cryogenic deposits of the east Arctic and Subarctic: Akademiy Nauk SSSR Far-East-Science Centre, 196 p. [In Russian.]

Velichko, A.A., Bogucki, A.B., Morozova, T.D., Udartsev, V.P., Khalcheva, T.A., and Tsatskin, A.I., 1984, Periglacial landscapes of the east European Plain, in Velichko, A.A., Wright, H.E., and Barnosky, C.W., eds., Late Quaternary environments of the Soviet Union: University of Minnesota Press, p. 94–118.

Veremeeva, A., and Gubin, S., 2009, Modern tundra landscapes of the Kolyma lowland and their evolution in the Holocene: Permafrost and Periglacial Processes, v. 20, p. 399–406.

von Toll, E., 1895, Die fossilen Eislager und ihreBeziehungenzu den Mammuthleichen —Wissenschaftliche Resultate des Yanalandes und der Neusibirischen Inseln [The fossil ice horizons and their correlation to mammoth remains—Scientific results from the Yana land and the New Siberian Islands]: - tersbourg, Imperatorskaja Akademija Nauk, v. 17, p. 1–86. [In German.]

Vtyurin, B.I., Grigoriev, N.F., Katasanov, E.M., Kuznetsova, T.P., Shvetsov, P.F., Shumsky, P.A., 1957, Local stratigraphic scheme of Quaternary deposits at the coast of the Laptev Sea: Proceedings of the interdepartmental council for the edition of an unified stratigraphical scheme of Siberia 1956, Report on the stratigraphy of Mesozoic and Cenozoic deposits, p. 564–572.

Walter, K.M., Edwards, M.E., Grosse, G., Zimov, S.A., and Chapin, F.S., III, 2007, Thermokarst lakes as a source of atmospheric CH_4 during the last deglaciation: Science, v. 318, p. 633–636.

Wetterich, S., Kuzmina, S., Andreev, A.A., Kienast, F., Meyer, H., Schirrmeister, L., Kuznetsova, T., and Sierralta, M., 2008, Palaeoenvironmental dynamics inferred from late Quaternary permafrost deposits on Kurungnakh Island, Lena Delta, northeast Siberia, Russia: Quaternary Science Reviews, v. 27, no. 15–16, p. 1523–1540.

Wetterich, S., Rudaya, N., Tumskoy, V., Andreev, A.A., Opel, T., Schirrmeister, L., and Meyer, H., 2011, Last Glacial Maximum records in permafrost of the East Siberian Arctic: Quaternary Science Reviews, v. 30, p. 3139–3151.

Zimov, S.A., Davydov, S.P., Zimova, G.M., Davydova, A.I., Schuur, E.A.G., Dutta, K., and Chapin, F.S., 2006b, Permafrost carbon—Stock and decomposability of a globally significant carbon pool: Geophysical Research Letters, v. 33, no. 20, L20502, 5 p.

Zimov, S.A., Schuur, E.A.G., and Chapin III, F.S., 2006a, Permafrost and the global carbon budget: Science, v. 312, p. 1612–1613.

Appendix A

List of Russian maps used for creating the digital database.

P-50-51 (Olekminsk)
> Rudenko, T.A., Matyushkov, A.D., Shurygin, A.G., Sai, T.S., and Feofanova, N.D., 1987, Map of Quaternary Deposits, P-50-51 (Olekminsk): ROSGEOLKOM, All-Russian Geological Research Institute VSEGEI, St. Petersburg, New Series, scale 1:1,000,000. (In Russian).

P-52-53 (Yakutsk)
> Kolpakov, V.V., 1992,Map of Quaternary Formations, P-52-53 (Yakutsk): Department of Natural Resources of the Russian Federation, Cartographic Company VSEGEI, St. Petersburg, New Series, scale 1:1,000,000. (In Russian).

Q-50-51 (Zhigansk)
> Kolpakov, V.V., 1986, Map of Quaternary Deposits, Q-50-51 (Zhigansk): Department of Geology of the U.S.S.R., All-Union Geological Research Institute VSEGEI, Leningrad, New Series, scale 1:1,000,000. (In Russian).

Q-52-53 (Verkhoyansk)
> Kolpakov, V.V., 1982, Map of Quaternary Deposits, Q-52-53 (Verkhoyansk): Department of Geology of the U.S.S.R., All-Union Geological Research Institute VSEGEI, Leningrad, New Series, scale 1:1,000,000. (In Russian).

Q-54-55 (Khonuu)
> Kolpakov, V.V., 1985, Map of Quaternary Deposits, Q-54-55 (Khonuu): Department of Geology of the U.S.S.R., All-Union Geological Research Institute VSEGEI, Leningrad, New Series, scale 1:1,000,000. (In Russian).

Q-56-57 (Srednekolymsk)
> Morozova, L.M., 1986, Map of Quaternary Deposits, Q-56-57 (Srednekolymsk), Department of Geology of the U.S.S.R., All-Union Geological Research Institute VSEGEI, Leningrad, New Series, scale 1:1,000,000. (In Russian).

R-53-(55) (Deputatsky)
> Kolpakov, V.V., 1990, Map of Quaternary Deposits, R-53-(55) (Deputatsky): Committee for Geology and Applied Mineral Resources of the Russian Federation, Cartographic Company VSEGEI, St. Petersburg, scale 1:1,000,000. (In Russian).

R-(55)-57 (Nizhnekolymsk)
> Ivanenko, G.V., 1998, Map of Quaternary Formations, R-(55)-57 (Nizhnekolymsk): Department of Natural Resources of the Russian Federation, Cartographic Company VSEGEI, St. Petersburg, New Series, scale 1:1,000,000. (In Russian).

S-47-49 (Ozero Taymyr)
> Bashlavin, D.K., and Borisova, T.P., 1988, Map of Quaternary Deposit, S-47-49 (Ozero Taymyr): Department of Natural Resources of the Russian Federation, Cartographic Company VSEGEI, St. Petersburg, New Series, scale 1:1,000,000. (In Russian).

S-50-52 (Bykovsky)
> Vanin, A.L., 2000, Map of Quaternary Formations, S-50-52 (Bykovsky): Department of Natural Resources of the Russian Federation, Cartographic Company VSEGEI, St. Petersburg New Series, scale 1:1,000,000. (In Russian).

S-53-55 (Novosibirskiye Ostrova)
> Ivanenko, G.V., 1995, Map of Quaternary Formations, S-53-55 (Novosibirskiye Ostrova): Department of Natural Resources of the Russian Federation, State scientific research enterprise Aerogeology. Cartographic Company VSEGEI, St. Petersburg, New Series, scale 1:1,000,000. (In Russian).

Appendix B

Table B1. Comparison of different Late Quaternary stratigraphies as used in the Quaternary Geology maps of Central and East Siberia with that of other regions and marine isotope stages (MIS). Comparisons are for approximate stratigraphical guidance. There may be local and regional differences for start and end of these periods.

		Code[a]	Central Siberia[b]	East Siberia[c]	East Siberian Mountains[d]	North America	Northern Europe	Global	MIS
Late Quaternary	Holocene	Q_{IV}	Holocene	Holocene	Holocene	Holocene	Holocene	Interglacial	MIS-1
	Late Pleistocene	Q_{III}^4	Sartan	Sartan	Second glaciation	Wisconsin Late	Weichselian Late	Glacial Stadial	MIS-2
		Q_{III}^3	Kargin	Kargin	Between glaciation	Wisconsin Middle	Weichselian Middle	Glacial Interstadial	MIS-3

Q_{III}^2	Muruktin	Zyryan	First glaciation	Early	Early	Stadial	MIS-4, 5a-d
Q_{III}^1	Kazantsev	Kazantsev	---	Sangamon	Eemian	Interglacial	MIS-5e

a – Stratigraphy in map tiles R-(55)-57, S-50-52,

b – Stratigraphy in map tiles P-52-53, S-47-49, P-50-51, Q-50-51

c – Stratigraphy in map tiles Q-52-53

d – Stratigraphy in map tiles Q-54-55, Q-56-57, R-53-(55), S-53-55

Appendix C

Table C1. Ground control points, projections, and resulting Root Mean Square (RMS) error from georeferencing the maps.

Map tile	Map name	Ground Control Points	RMS Error	Projection
P-50-51	Olekminsk	21	302 m	GK 20N, Pulkovo 1942
P-52-53	Yakutsk	33	236 m	GK 22N, Pulkovo 1942
Q-50-51	Zhigansk	20	225 m	GK 20N,Pulkovo 1942
Q-52-53	Verkhoyansk	41	142 m	GK 22N, Pulkovo 1942
Q-54-55	Khonuu	21	205 m	GK 24N, Pulkovo 1942
Q-56-57	Srednekolymsk	21	175 m	GK 26N, Pulkovo 1942
R-53-(55)	Deputatsky	58	189 m	GK 24N, Pulkovo 1942
R-(55)-57	Nizhnekolymsk	n.a.[1]	n.a.[1]	GK 26N, Pulkovo 1942
S-47-49	Ozero Taymyr	50	257 m	GK 18N, Pulkovo 1942
S-50-52	Bykovsky	70	137 m	GK 21N, Pulkovo 1942
S-53-55	Novosibirskiye Ostrova	71	127 m	GK 24N, Pulkovo 1942

[1] Rectification data was not available for this map but is assumed to be similar as for the other map tiles.

Appendix D

Table D1. Geologic units in each map tile interpreted as late Pleistocene syngenetic, ice-rich Yedoma deposits.

Map tile	Geological unit according to map				
	Unit code	Lithogenetic type	Stratigraphy	Ground ice signature	
				Map view	Cross-profile view
P-50-51	LIIImr-sr	Loess	$Q_{III}^2 - Q_{III}^4$	Ice-rich	Ice-rich
P-52-53	LIIIsr	Loess (cryogenic-eolian deposits)	Q_{III}^4	Ice-rich	Syngenetic ice wedges
P-52-53	LIIImr-sr	Loess (cryogenic-eolian deposits)	$Q_{III}^2 - Q_{III}^4$	Ice-rich[a]	-
P-52-53	I,LIIImr-sr	Lacustrine and cryogenic-eolian genesis	$Q_{III}^2 - Q_{III}^4$	Ice-rich	Syngenetic ice wedges
Q-50-51	LIIImr,sr	Loess, cryogenic-eolian genesis	$Q_{III}^2 - Q_{III}^4$	Ice-rich	Syngenetic ice wedges
Q-50-51	LIIIsr	Loess, cryogenic-eolian genesis	Q_{III}^4	Ice-rich	Syngenetic ice wedges
Q-52-53	kvIIIz-sr	Cryogenic-eolian ice-rich deposits	$Q_{III}^2 - Q_{III}^4$	-	Syngenetic ice wedges
Q-54-55	LIII2-4	Loess	$Q_{III}^2 - Q_{III}^4$	Ice-rich	Syngenetic ice wedges
Q-54-55	LIII4	Loess	Q_{III}^4	Ice-rich	Syngenetic ice wedges
Q-56-57	LIII2+4	Loess-like cryogenic-eolian, lacustrine-bog, and lacustrine-alluvial deposits	Q_{III}^2, Q_{III}^4	Ice-rich	Syngenetic ice wedges
R-53-(55)	LIII2-4	Loess (cryogenic-eolian deposits)	$Q_{III}^2 - Q_{III}^4$	Ice-rich	Syngenetic ice wedges
R-53-(55)	d,LIII2-4	Deluvial, loess (cryogenic-eolian deposits)	$Q_{III}^2 - Q_{III}^4$	Ice-rich	Syngenetic ice wedges
R-(55)-57	LIII2-4	Loess-like lacustrine-alluvial	$Q_{III}^2 - Q_{III}^4$	Ice-rich	Syngenetic ice wedges
R-(55)-57	LdsIII2-4	Loess-like deluvial-solifluction deposits	$Q_{III}^2 - Q_{III}^4$	Ice-rich	-
S-47-49	lIIIkr-sr	Lacustrine	$Q_{III}^3 - Q_{III}^4$	Ice-rich[a]	Syngenetic ice wedges
S-47-49	lIIIsr	Lacustrine	Q_{III}^4	Ice-rich[a]	Syngenetic ice wedges
S-47-49	aIIIsr	Alluvial	Q_{III}^4	Ice-rich[a]	Syngenetic ice wedges
S-47-49	laIIImr-sr	Lacustrine-alluvial	$Q_{III}^2 - Q_{III}^4$	Ice-rich	Syngenetic ice wedges
S-47-49	laIIIkr-sr	Lacustrine-alluvial	$Q_{III}^3 - Q_{III}^4$	Ice-rich	Syngenetic ice wedges
S-47-49	laIIIkr	Lacustrine-alluvial	Q_{III}^3	Ice-rich[a]	Syngenetic ice wedges
S-47-49	laIIIsr	Lacustrine-alluvial	Q_{III}^4	Ice-rich	Syngenetic ice wedges
S-50-52	KIII2-4	Cryogenic complex origins	$Q_{III}^2 - Q_{III}^4$	Ice-rich	-
S-53-55	KIII2-4	Cryogenic lacustrine-alluvial	$Q_{III}^2 - Q_{III}^4$	Ice-rich	Syngenetic ice wedges
S-53-55	KII-III	Cryogenic lacustrine-alluvial	$Q_{II} - Q_{III}$ not differentiated	Ice-rich	Syngenetic ice wedges

[a] In this unit some polygons lack ice-rich signatures in the map view, while other polygons of the same unit have an ice-rich signature. Our map includes all these polygons as Yedoma

24